PANDAS

LIVING WILD

LIVING WILD

Published by Creative Education
P.O. Box 227, Mankato, Minnesota 56002
Creative Education is an imprint of The Creative Company
www.thecreativecompany.us

Design and production by Mary Herrmann
Art direction by Rita Marshall
Printed by Corporate Graphics in the United States of America

Photographs by 123RF (Rick Carlson, Alexander Muntean), Alamy (Danita Delimont, Nick Greaves, Imagebroker, Photos 12, Inga Spence), Corbis (Bettmann, NIR ELIAS/Reuters), Dreamstime (Kitchner Bain, Benjshepherd, Carmentianya, Eric Gevaert, Jennie Magro, Mike711, Xiaobin Qui, Ron Sumners, Tang Yu), Getty Images (Yang Enuo/ChinaFotoPress, Inga Spence/Visuals Unlimited, Inc., Chip Somodevilla, STR/AFP, Keren Su), iStockphoto (Dirk Freder, Richard Laurence, Peter Niesen)

Library of Congress Cataloging-in-Publication Data
Gish, Melissa.
Pandas / by Melissa Gish.
p. cm. — (Living wild)
Includes bibliographical references and index.
Summary: A look at pandas, including their habitats, physical characteristics such as their black-and-white fur, behaviors, relationships with humans, and threatened status in the world today.
ISBN 978-1-60818-082-0
1. Giant panda—Juvenile literature. I. Title.

QL737.C27G53 2011
599.789—dc22   2010028311

CPSIA: 020212 PO1534

9 8 7 6 5 4 3 2

c CREATIVE EDUCATION

PANDAS

Melissa Gish

As the sun rises over the mountaintops in southwestern China, a cool mist drapes itself

over the bamboo forest in the Tangjiahe Nature Reserve.

As the sun rises over the mountaintops in southwestern China, a cool mist drapes itself over the bamboo forest in the Tangjiahe Nature Reserve. An 18-month-old panda follows his mother through the dense greenery. The mother panda looks back and lets out a series of snorts. Now pregnant with a new cub, she turns away from her offspring. The young panda, bleating, follows, but the mother turns her body

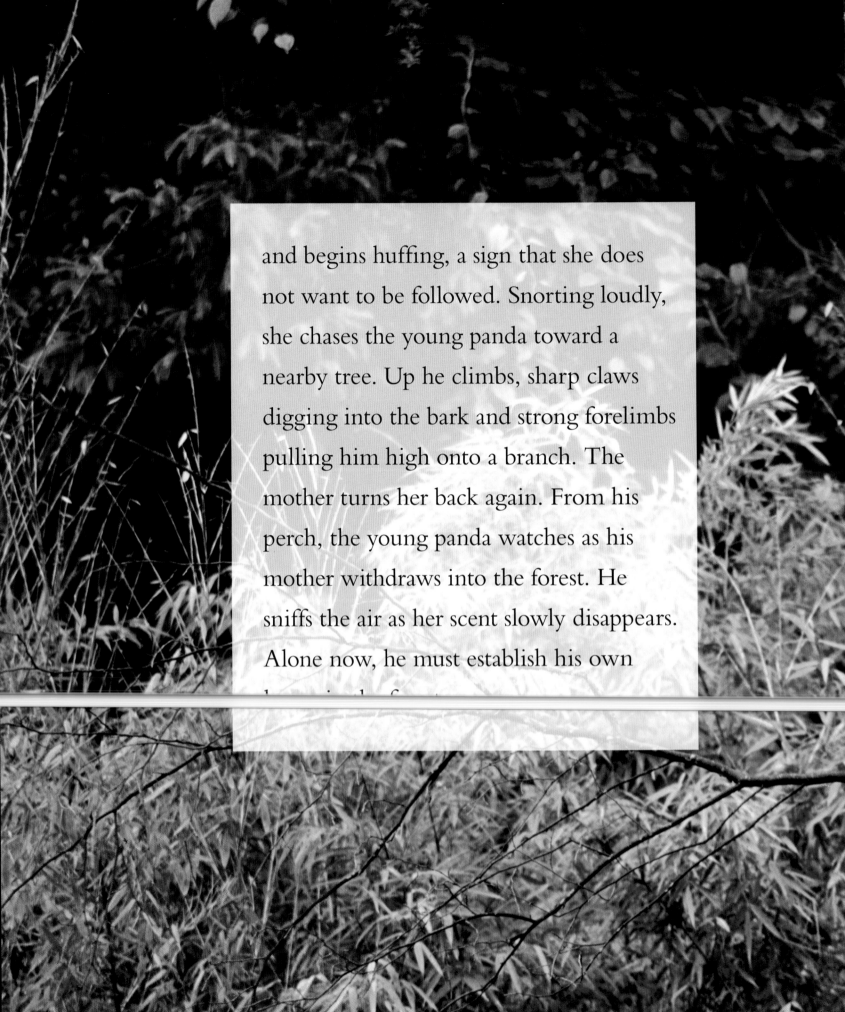

and begins huffing, a sign that she does not want to be followed. Snorting loudly, she chases the young panda toward a nearby tree. Up he climbs, sharp claws digging into the bark and strong forelimbs pulling him high onto a branch. The mother turns her back again. From his perch, the young panda watches as his mother withdraws into the forest. He sniffs the air as her scent slowly disappears. Alone now, he must establish his own

WHERE IN THE WORLD THEY LIVE

Once widespread throughout Asia, the single species of giant panda is now confined to small areas of bamboo forest in central and southwestern China. The colored squares represent the locations of pandas living in Sichuan, Shaanxi, and Gansu provinces.

■ **Giant Panda**
China

BAMBOO BEARS

The giant panda is one of the rarest animals on Earth. Five varieties of panda **evolved** about three million years ago, but now only one species remains. Today's giant panda (*Ailuropoda melanoleuca*) is twice as big as its earliest known ancestor, the pygmy giant panda, whose two-million-year-old fossilized skull was discovered in China in 2007. Several thousand years ago, pandas lived throughout China and Southeast Asia, but today, fewer than 1,600 wild pandas inhabit just 6 isolated areas of central and southwestern China.

Pandas are mammals. All mammals, with the exceptions of the platypus and hedgehog-like echidna, give birth to live offspring and produce milk to feed their young. Mammals are warm-blooded animals. This means that they are able to keep their body temperature at a constant level, no matter what the temperature is outside. The panda's thick fur keeps it warm in its cold mountain habitat. Pandas prefer low temperatures and high humidity, so they establish winter home ranges in cool, rainy habitats between 5,000 and 7,000 feet (1,524–2,134 m) and move to snowy home ranges at higher elevations—some as high

The skin under a panda's black fur is nearly black, but the skin under its white fur is pink in color.

The sun bear of Southeast Asia, also known as the honey bear, is the smallest member of the bear family.

In China, panda relatives are known by different names: brown bears are horse bears, and sun bears are dog bears.

as 11,500 feet (3,505 m)—in summer. The average home range covers an area of two square miles (5.2 sq km).

Pandas are white with black ears, muzzles, legs, and shoulders. They also have black eye patches. Scientists once believed that this distinctive black-and-white coloring made pandas related to raccoons, but it is now known that pandas belong to the Ursidae, or bear, family. The closest living relatives of bears are the pinnipeds, a group that includes seals, sea lions, and walruses. Bears and pinnipeds share a common ancestor that lived more than 20 million years ago. Besides pandas, there are seven other species of bear: sun bears, sloth bears, brown bears, polar bears, spectacled bears, and American and Asiatic black bears.

The Latin word for "bear," *ursus*, was also used to name the constellations Ursa Major and Ursa Minor—Great Bear and Little Bear. In English, the word "bear" originated from *bher*, which means "glossy brown" in an eastern European language that was spoken more than 2,000 years ago. This word was used to describe the brown bears that were abundant in the Carpathian Mountains in what are now the countries of Slovakia, Ukraine, and Romania.

Pandas are one of the smallest bear species. Unlike brown

Pandas walk and climb like other bears, but their coloration sets them apart from their closest relatives.

Red pandas use their tails as blankets in their cold, mountain habitats of Nepal, Myanmar, and central China.

bears and polar bears, which can grow to be 8 or 9 feet (2.4 or 2.7 m) long and weigh 900 pounds (408 kg) or more than 1,000 pounds (454 kg) respectively, male pandas average no more than 6 feet (1.8 m) in length and weigh up to 240 pounds (109 kg). Female pandas are about 10 to 20 percent smaller than males, averaging about 200 pounds (91 kg).

Unlike other bears, whose eyes have round pupils, pandas have vertical, slit-like pupils similar to those of cats. For this reason, the Chinese commonly call the panda *dah xiong mao* (*da SHOWNG mow*), or "great bear cat." The source of the word "panda" is not known, but historians believe that *nigalya ponya*, a Nepalese term meaning "eater of bamboo" that was used to describe the red panda—a small, catlike mammal not classified as a true panda—may have provided the foundation.

All bears are omnivores, meaning they eat both meat and plants, but pandas do not usually choose to consume meat. Apart from the occasional bamboo rat, 99 percent of a panda's diet is made up of certain varieties of bamboo, the woody grass known as the fastest-growing plant on Earth. Pandas also eat flowers, vines, and some other grasses if they happen upon them, but they prefer to find

Like giant pandas, red pandas have an elongated wrist bone, which helps them grip bamboo as they feed.

Unlike other animals capable of eating meat, pandas have teeth that more closely resemble those of grass-eating animals such as cattle.

a spot surrounded by bamboo in which to sit and munch for up to 16 hours a day, taking naps between meals.

Pandas have 21 pairs of teeth, 2 pairs of which are sharp canines. Pandas can consume the hard stems of mature bamboo as easily as the leaves and young bamboo shoots. They break the tall stalks of bamboo into pieces about 10 to 16 inches (25–41 cm) long and begin eating them from the middle toward the top—the tenderest part. If they are still hungry after that, pandas will eat the lower part, which is woodier and tougher to chew. They must use their strong back teeth, called molars, and sharp claws to strip away the hard bark to reach the soft inside part.

A panda's jaws are strong, and its molars are extra wide—a perfect combination for grinding up bamboo. A panda needs to chew only about six times before swallowing. Bamboo is a good source of the **nutrient** protein, but because the food is low in calories, a panda needs to consume a lot of bamboo—up to 84 pounds (38 kg) every day—to generate enough energy for its body to function properly.

Unlike other species of bear that **hibernate** during part or all of the winter, when food sources typically dwindle, the panda remains constantly active, because its main food

Giant pandas are the only living members of the bear family that can survive by feeding exclusively on plants.

A panda establishing a home range needs to have access to a water source that is within half a mile (0.8 km).

source grows year round. While rain and snow can cause the humidity level to exceed 80 percent, the panda is well equipped for this damp but chilly climate. Its skin secretes an oily substance that coats the dense fur, protecting the panda from cold and keeping its skin dry.

Like their relatives the polar bears, pandas have thick fur around their toes and footpads to insulate their paws and prevent ice from building up. One thing that only pandas have on their front paws is an extra-long wrist bone, called an elongated radial sesamoid, which works like a short thumb. Combined with their five clawed digits, this additional feature allows pandas to hold items as slender as a pencil.

Pandas have a strong sense of smell, which they use to detect each other in the forest. Because they are solitary animals and prefer to avoid each other, except during mating season, when males seek out females. Pandas seem to never be in a hurry to get anywhere. Like other bears, pandas roll their shoulders and hips when they walk. This movement is called a diagonal walk. But unlike their relatives, pandas seldom run, choosing instead to walk quickly when escaping a threat.

Due to their remote habitats, few scientifically significant studies of wild pandas have been conducted.

*Pandas often like to rest in the crook
of a tall tree's branches and are
surprisingly agile for their size.*

Fewer than 2,000 dholes
exist in fragmented habitats
in Russian, Indian, and Asian
forests and jungles.

W andering through small areas of forest in southwestern and central China in search of the sweetest,
ripest bamboo shoots, pandas do little more
throughout their lives than eat and rest. They may
live to be 20 years old in the wild, and captive pandas can
live up to 10 years longer. Pandas never get a full night's sleep
because they eat for about eight hours and then rest for about
four before starting to eat again. An adult panda may sit on
its rump, leaning its back against a tree, and eat all of the
ripe bamboo within its reach over a period of several hours.

The only predators that pandas may occasionally
encounter are leopards and wild dogs called dholes
(*DOLZ*). Pandas share their forest homes with smaller
creatures, including hog badgers, palm civets, weasels,
and bamboo rats. The bamboo rats compete with
pandas for food by uprooting young bamboo plants and
dragging them into their underground burrows. Pandas,
particularly pregnant ones in need of extra calories and
protein, have been known to eat these rodents.

Female pandas can become pregnant during only three
days each year, in late April. This is one reason the species

is so rare. Another is that panda populations are highly fragmented, so the bears have a difficult time locating each other during mating season. When a female is ready to mate, she will rub her hindquarters against trees and rocks, leaving scent markers that tell other pandas about her. The scent, which is produced by glands in her body, reveals her gender, age, and breeding condition.

Male pandas leave scent markers as well, letting females know where available males may be found and warning other males about their competition. Male pandas will do a handstand, lifting themselves up on their front paws and rubbing their lower bodies against trees and rocks, to leave scent markers. The higher the scent marker, the taller the panda appears, which is meant to both intimidate other males and attract females.

Recent research conducted by Georgia's Zoo Atlanta revealed that pandas also vocalize during mating season. Males and females have distinct voices, and adult pandas make a variety of sounds—including bleats, barks, growls, and squeals—to tell about themselves and to let pandas of the opposite gender know that they are searching for a mate. Males vocalize to reveal their size, which is an

important consideration for females choosing a mate and males deciding whether to fight other—perhaps larger—males for the chance to mate with a female. Female pandas' vocalizations reveal their age, which is also a valuable bit of information, since males find older females, who may be experienced mothers, to be more desirable mates.

Once a male has located a suitable female, he will begin to play-fight with her, gently biting her and wrestling with her. This rough play helps the pair bond with one another. Because mating pandas expend a great

Pandas are extremely playful and have been known to approach domestic pigs and sheep out of curiosity.

Mother pandas lick their babies to calm them down, which helps them pass feces or urine from their bodies.

deal of energy, the pair must stop frequently to eat and rest between bouts of play. Once the female has been impregnated, the male panda returns to his solitary home range and leaves the female to give birth and **rear** the offspring alone. Baby pandas develop inside their mothers for about five months before being born. In preparation for the birth, the female selects a secluded den site, usually in the cavity of an enormous tree stump or in a natural limestone cave. This will be her offspring's home for the first six to seven months of its life.

A newborn panda, called a cub, weighs just 4 ounces (113 g) and is nearly 1,000 times smaller than its mother. About half of all panda births result in twins. A mother panda cannot care for two cubs, however, and must choose just one, leaving the other to die. Cubs are born with only a sparse coat of thin, white fur on their bodies, causing them to appear hairless. The mother holds her tiny cub against her chest to keep it warm and let it nurse on the nourishing milk her body provides. She will remain in the den for the first five or six days after giving birth, foregoing food and water to provide warmth and security for her newborn.

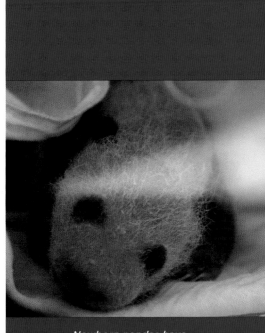

Newborn pandas have voracious appetites and cry for milk at intervals of approximately two hours.

A panda cub is unable to regulate its body temperature, which must remain at about 97 °F (36 °C), so it relies on its mother to keep warm. When the mother leaves the den to feed, she does not linger, hurrying back within hours. After about six weeks, the cub—now more than double its birth size—opens its eyes, and three to four weeks later, it begins crawling around the den. At about 10 weeks of age, its fluffy black-and-white fur develops. Four weeks later, the cub's teeth emerge, but it is not yet ready to eat bamboo. While the mother takes longer breaks away from the den to feed, she still returns frequently to nurse her cub.

By the time the cub is five months old, it has become a miniature version of its mother. With thick fur and steady legs, it walks well and plays with its mother, climbing trees and rolling down its mother's back. When the cub is six to seven months old, the mother leads it out of the den to explore the forest, and she introduces the cub to water and bamboo. A panda mother remains protective of her cub for the next 12 to 14 months. By then, the cub—nearly 2 years old and weighing about 120 pounds (54 kg)—is independent and can forage for its own food.

Its mother then rejects it, as she must prepare for the next breeding season and a new cub.

The young panda will establish a home range near its mother's. Well prepared by its mother, it will climb trees to avoid predators such as leopards and select the best bamboo for feeding. It will remain playful and curious for the first few years of its life, perhaps doubling its weight as it develops into an adult panda. When the panda is fully mature, it will be ready to have cubs of its own. Males mature around age seven and females around six.

The order in which a panda's teeth appear varies among cubs, with some getting their front teeth before their back teeth.

DESCRIPTION OF THE PANDA

They had not deceived our missionary on the subject of the existence of white bears in the most inaccessible mountains. Abbe David made haste to interrogate the huntsmen, and he received from them the promise that some skins of the curious animal would soon be brought to him. In fact, he was not long in being put in possession of the huge mammifer [mammal], at once remarkable by singular characteristics of form and by its altogether exceptional colour. The animal, of the common size of bears, is white, with the ears, the surroundings of the eyes, the four members, and the tip of the tail, black: the ears are short and the soles of the feet well provided with hair. A naturalist ought always to fear to attach too much importance to colours, and this distrust is especially well founded when black and white are concerned; but some individuals of different ages having been taken, it is certain that the vestment of this famous carnivorous animal of Mou-pin is truly characteristic. If the animal, which has the aspect and proportions of the bear, belongs really to this genus of mammifers, the acquisition of a species having a physiognomy [features] so special, would already present much interest; but here the discovery is precious on other grounds; we have the representative of a type altogether new, which is separated from our bears by the form of the skeleton and by the dentition and its approximation to the American rat, or more especially to the [red] panda of the mountains of Central Asia, whose size, however, hardly exceeds that of the cat.

by Father Armand David (1826–1900), excerpt from Natural History of North China

"PANDA"MONIUM

During his 3 trips to China, Father Armand David recorded 63 animal species previously unknown to science.

C onsidered national treasures in China, pandas have traditionally been used as gifts by Chinese leaders. The earliest account of such an exchange occurred in the year A.D. 685, when Chinese empress Wu Zetian gave pandas to the Japanese emperor as a token of peace. But the panda was viewed as a different kind of treasure by the Europeans who first encountered them. Europeans began traveling in great numbers to China in the late 1800s. After priest and **zoologist** Father Armand David (*dah-VEED*) encountered pandas in 1869, he wrote about them in his book, *Natural History of North China*, which was published in 1873.

David's book and other reports of pandas in China captured the interest of big-game hunters. The elusive animals were much sought after by hunters in the late 19th and early 20th centuries. When two sons of former United States president Theodore Roosevelt shot two giant pandas and sent them to Chicago's Field Museum in 1929, the gifts were not received with gratitude. Unlike other specimens of wild animals at the museum, such as tigers, wolves, and leopards, which struck people as ferocious and deadly creatures, pandas were viewed as cute, cuddly animals undeserving of such a fate. Public outcry led to a new activity: the hunt for live pandas. People wanted to see pandas romping around in zoos, not stuffed with sawdust and displayed in museum dioramas.

The first panda in North America arrived in 1937. Named Su Lin, the bear was exhibited at the Brookfield Zoo in Chicago and was followed the next year by pandas at New York's Bronx Zoo, then a panda named Happy at the St. Louis Zoo in 1939. Since then, dozens of pandas have gone on exhibit at zoos around the world, where they continue to be monitored by the Chinese government. In 1972, China presented a pair of pandas named Ling-Ling and Hsing-Hsing as official state gifts to U.S. president Richard Nixon; they were housed at the National Zoo in Washington, D.C. During their lifetime, the pair had five cubs, but none lived for more than a few days.

Until recently, most captive pandas did not live long and did not have surviving offspring, as zookeepers knew too little about these animals to provide them with proper nutrition and activities. Today, however, researchers have made a science out of the keeping and **captive breeding**

of giant pandas. One of the most successful institutions is the San Diego Zoo, home to the world-famous Giant Panda Research Station, which serves to not only exhibit pandas but help them breed as well.

Research on panda health, growth, and reproduction at San Diego began in 1996 with two pandas on an extended loan from the Chinese government, Bai Yun and Shi Shi. In 1999, Bai Yun gave birth to Hua Mei, the first giant panda born in North America to survive

A cub named Mei-Mei was brought from China to be a companion for the Brookfield Zoo's Su Lin in 1938.

In The Amazing Panda Adventure, *the main character, Ryan, names the panda cub after his best friend, Johnny.*

to adulthood. Four years later, Bai Yun gave birth to Mei Sheng. Both cubs, along with their father, Shi Shi, were then sent to China in exchange for Gao Gao, another male to breed with Bai Yun. The San Diego Zoo—which in 2010 had four adults and young Yun Zi, a fifth Bai Yun cub—houses the most pandas of any zoo in the U.S. Visitors to the San Diego Zoo Web site can watch the pandas on the zoo's live Panda Cam stream.

Pandas are some of the most recognizable and loved of all wild animals. Their image has been adopted as a logo or mascot by a variety of organizations, from the Panda Express restaurant chain to the World Wildlife Fund to the University of Alberta in Edmonton women's sports teams, the Pandas. A panda named Jing Jing served as one of the mascots of the 2008 Summer Olympics, which were held in Beijing, China. Even online role-playing games recognize the appeal of pandas. The highly popular *World of Warcraft* series has incorporated a fictitious ethnic group called the Pandaren, humanoid pandas with a love of nature and a desire for peace among all races of characters in the game.

In motion pictures, pandas have appeared in real form, as robotic puppets, and as animated characters. In

Pandas must eat a lot of food because they digest and metabolize only about 17 percent of the plant matter that they consume.

Kung Fu Panda was so popular it spawned a movie sequel, TV show, video game, books, and toys.

the 1995 film *The Amazing Panda Adventure*, shots of live pandas were combined with animatronics to tell the story of a boy vacationing in China who gets caught up in a Chinese girl's plan to rescue a baby panda from **poachers** bent on killing the mother panda and selling the cub. The film was shot on location in Chengdu, China, home of the Chengdu Panda Base, a panda research center. In 2001, the IMAX movie *China: The Panda Adventure* was also filmed in China using trained and wild pandas.

Perhaps the most popular movie panda is Po of DreamWorks Animation's *Kung Fu Panda* (2008). Po dreams of becoming a great martial artist, but he lacks confidence and self-discipline. Accepted by a great teacher of martial arts, a red panda named Master Shifu, Po learns the skills he needs to achieve his dream and become the Dragon Warrior. A related short film, *Kung Fu Panda: The Secrets of the Furious Five*, was released on DVD in 2008, and a feature-length sequel, *Kung Fu Panda: The Kaboom of Doom* (2011), invites moviegoers to join the continuing adventures of Po and his kung fu comrades.

The Panda Who Would Not Eat (2008) is a picture book by Ruth Todd Evans about one of the first pandas

to arrive at the San Diego Zoo. The true story tells of the difficulty keepers had in getting the panda to eat until the problem was solved with help from one of the zoo's neighbors. The Quail Botanical Gardens, which changed its name to the San Diego Botanic Garden in 2009, provided the zoo with different kinds of bamboo from its unique bamboo garden. Some of the bamboo turned out to be just what the pandas wanted. Now, the San Diego Botanic Garden and the San Diego Zoo both grow bamboo that is fed to the pandas at the zoo.

The San Diego Zoo's Zoo Corps program enlists teenagers in teaching visitors about animals and conservation.

Doctors and scientists at China's Chengdu Panda Base are dedicated to providing pandas with the best possible care.

PANDAS ON THE BRINK

While the number of wild pandas has increased slightly in recent years—thanks to new protective laws—scientists believe that wild pandas may never reach sustainable numbers, which would lead to **extinction** of the species. Pandas have a very small window of time during which they can mate each year, and fragmentation of their habitat makes it difficult for individuals to reach each other in time. Those pandas that do mate rear only one cub. Such obstacles limit the potential for wild panda populations to increase. Even if panda populations did recover, there would not be enough land to sustain them, as wild bamboo forests have largely been **deforested** for urban and agricultural development.

Because pandas seem to lose their instinct for breeding when living in captivity, in China, the captive rearing of pandas is serious business. China's Sichuan Giant Panda Sanctuaries is a complex of seven major panda research centers responsible for about one-third of the world's panda population. The largest of these facilities is the Panda Research Center in the Wolong National Nature Reserve, which is home to nearly 100 captive pandas. More than 60 cubs have

According to Chinese tradition, panda cubs born in captivity should not be named until they are 100 days old.

been born at the center since its establishment in 1963.

In May 2008, a major earthquake struck the Sichuan province, devastating the Panda Research Center at Wolong. Several pandas were injured, and one was killed. The center's pandas were moved to safe locations while the facility underwent reconstruction. The new center is located in the town of Huangcaoping, about six miles (9.7 km) from the destroyed facility. The San Diego Zoo partnered with Wolong to help fund the project.

Another Chinese center, the Chengdu Panda Base, is considered one of the top facilities in the world. What started with 6 pandas rescued from the wild has turned into China's premier panda research center, housing more than 60 pandas. More than 100 cubs have been born at Chengdu, which loans its pandas to zoos in several countries, including the U.S., England, and Japan. The details of each panda's birth are recorded so that the greatest **genetic** diversity can be achieved in all breeding programs around the world.

Important research on such aspects of panda life as behavior, diet, and reproduction is conducted at all zoos and research facilities where pandas live. Animal behavior

Although wild pandas are accustomed to leading solitary lives, those kept in captivity get along well together.

By observing panda behavior, zookeepers can also determine what physical features should be included in an exhibit.

specialists create a complete list of repeated behaviors exhibited by a particular species. This list of behaviors is called an ethogram. The first panda ethogram of 70 behaviors was created at Washington, D.C.'s National Zoo by biologist Devra Kleiman in 1983. Since then, the panda ethogram has grown to include many more observed behaviors. From such studies, researchers are able to make comparisons between captive panda behavior and wild panda behavior.

For example, wild pandas must forage for food for up to 10 hours a day, but captive pandas, which are fed a more nutritious diet, need to forage only about 4 hours per day. This leaves them plenty of time for play. Scientists who study animal behavior develop enrichment strategies—

using toys, architecture, puzzles, and other objects—to improve the psychological well-being of captive animals. Pandas are naturally curious and, even as adults, will play with objects such as rubber balls and food dispensers.

In addition to generous amounts of fresh bamboo, captive pandas are fed a special mix of soybeans, ground bamboo, eggs, flour, corn, vitamins, and minerals that is shaped into small, hard loaves called *wowotou*. Captive pandas are also given blocks of ice with carrots and yams frozen in them. These treats not only allow pandas to cool down during warm weather, but they also stimulate the pandas' problem-solving skills by challenging the bears to free the embedded vegetables.

Scientists agree that the most important reason for keeping pandas in captivity is to breed them. One of the most valuable discoveries made in the field of captive breeding was the concept of twin-swapping. Until recently, human caregivers could not keep captive newborns that had been abandoned by their mothers alive for more than a few days. Then it was found that if the keepers switched the twins every few days so that each was able to nurse, the mother panda did not seem

Environmental enrichment activities allow captive animals to demonstrate a variety of natural behaviors.

to notice that she was caring for two different cubs. The practice of twin-swapping means that both twins have an equal chance of surviving to maturity.

Because their natural habitat continues to shrink, pandas may be beyond saving in the wild, but scientists hope to keep pandas on the planet as long as possible. A more difficult attempt at conservation that is being tried is **cloning**. In 1999, a team of scientists at the Chinese Academy of Science's Institute of Zoology successfully produced a panda **embryo** by putting the **DNA** of a panda into the egg of a rabbit. Three years later, these scientists discovered a way to implant a panda embryo into the body of a female cat. While the cat was not able to give birth to a panda cub, the experiment was a first step toward using other animals to carry and give birth to panda cubs. Research to find a suitable replacement mother to carry a baby panda continues, but scientists warn that cloning technology is still in its very early stages of development, and the fate of pandas is too unsure to rely on cloning to save the species. For now, captive panda programs are the bears' best chance for survival.

Most captive-reared pandas remain in captivity their entire lives. Some have been returned to the wild, but most of those could not survive—either starving or dying from fights with wild pandas over territory. This makes the rebuilding of wild panda populations extremely difficult. Pandas are dangerously close to extinction. They struggle against the effects of environmental change and human interference from poaching and deforestation. While researchers remain optimistic, continued large-scale habitat conservation and reclamation efforts are critical to providing these remarkable animals with safe and lasting places to live on our planet.

In 2011, Chinese researchers launched a two-year census of wild pandas, cataloging panda DNA from feces samples.

ANIMAL TALE: THE PANDA'S MARKINGS

For centuries, the dense bamboo forests of southwestern Sichuan province have figured prominently in Chinese culture. This ancient folk tale tells how the panda, an important member of the bamboo forest's ecosystem, got its unique markings.

Long ago, there were no pandas, only white bears called *bai xiong*. They lived in the bamboo forests of Sichuan and spent their days eating bamboo and playing games. One day, a little girl, the daughter of a poor farmer, wandered into the bamboo forest and came across a *bai xiong* cub. The cub and the girl regarded each other with curiosity, and then, without a word, they began to chase each other playfully through the bamboo. The cub's mother watched from a distance, certain that the girl meant her cub no harm. And so the girl and the cub spent the entire day playing together. When night fell, the cub and his mother walked the girl home to her village.

For many days after, the little girl returned to the forest to play with the cub, and they became great friends. The mother bear was pleased with this friendship, for she could spend her days leisurely munching on bamboo shoots, knowing that her cub was safely playing nearby with the little girl.

One day while they were playing in the bamboo forest, the little girl and the cub heard a strange sound, like someone coughing. This sound grew louder, and the little girl and the cub decided they should find the mother bear. Just as they turned to head down the path

toward the mother bear's favorite feeding area, a leopard burst out of the bushes and crouched before them, huffing and coughing as leopards do when they are aggravated.

The leopard suddenly leaped upon the cub, who cried out in terror. The little girl immediately picked up a rock and threw it at the leopard. The mother bear heard her cub's cry and came rushing up the path. But she was too late. The leopard had turned away from the cub and leaped on the little girl, knocking her to the ground and crushing her. The mother bear barked at the leopard, baring her sharp teeth, and the leopard ran away.

Heartbroken over the little girl's death, the mother bear and her cub began to cry. Soon all of the bears of the forest had gathered around the little girl's body and listened to the cub explain how the girl had sacrificed her life to save his. All of the bears cried out and tore at the ground with their paws in great sadness. As they wiped their mud-stained paws across their weeping eyes, black spots stained their faces. The bears wailed and hugged each other, wiping their muddy paws across each other's backs. This left black stains around their midsections. As the crying grew louder, they covered their ears with their paws to shut out the sadness, leaving black stains on their ears.

Upon this great outpouring of grief, the *bai xiong* ceased to exist. They had become *xiong mao*, giant pandas, and to this day they have continued to wear their dark colors as a sign of mourning for the brave little girl who gave her life to save her friend, the cub.

GLOSSARY

captive breeding – being bred and raised in a place from which escape is not possible

cloning – the scientific process of creating an identical copy of a living organism

deforested – cleared trees away from a forest

DNA – deoxyribonucleic acid; a substance found in every living thing that determines the species and individual characteristics of that thing

ecosystem – a community of organisms that live together in an environment

embryo – an unborn or unhatched offspring in its early stages of development

evolved – gradually developed into a new form

extinction – the act or process of becoming extinct; coming to an end or dying out

genetic – relating to genes, the basic physical units of heredity

hibernate – to spend the winter in a sleeplike state in which breathing and heart rate slow down

metabolize – to conduct the processes that keep a body alive, including making use of food for energy

nutrient – a substance that gives an animal energy and helps it grow

poachers – people who hunt protected species of wild animals, even though doing so is against the law

rear – to bring up and care for a child or young animal until it is fully grown

zoologist – a person who studies animals and their lives

SELECTED BIBLIOGRAPHY

Angel, Heather. *Panda: An Intimate Portrait of One of the World's Most Elusive Characters*. London: David & Charles, 2008.

Chengdu Research Base of Giant Panda Breeding. "Homepage." Chengdu Panda Base. http://www.panda.org.cn/english/index.htm.

Lindberg, Donald, and Karen Baragona. *Giant Pandas: Biology and Conservation*. Berkeley: University of California Press, 2004.

Lumpkin, Susan, and John Seidensticker. *Smithsonian Book of Giant Pandas*. Washington, D.C.: Smithsonian Institution Press, 2002.

Maple, Terry L. *Saving the Giant Panda*. Atlanta: Longstreet Press, 2000.

San Diego Zoo. "Panda Cam." http://www.sandiegozoo.org/pandacam/index.html.

Young pandas may climb trees to escape predators or to avoid confrontations with larger, more aggressive pandas.

INDEX